Brunette and Boozy Free

Samantha Holsomback

Copyright © 2025

All Rights Reserved

Dedication

To my children

Acknowledgment

To my beautiful children, whose unwavering love fueled my inspiration, strength, and determination.

Special thanks to my husband for your endless support with innumerable insightful conversations.

Deep gratitude to my mother, whose own perseverance in life serves as my brilliant guiding star.

To my cherished friends, whose encouragement proved invaluable along my journey, and to God for filling my heart with peace and my mind with purpose.

Finally, to my publishing team, for their keen eye and guidance in shaping this manuscript through late nights and countless revisions.

Table of Contents

Dedication iii
Acknowledgment iv
About the Author vi
Chapter 1 The Ripple Effect 1
Chapter 2 Embracing Your Inner Evolution 8
Chapter 3 The Devil is a Glass of Wine 15
Chapter 4 From Cheers to Tears 23
Chapter 5 Beyond the Glamour 30
Chapter 6 Embracing A New Life Without Alcohol 37
Chapter 7 Boundaries, Growth, and Letting Go 45
Chapter 8 The Power of Change and Self-Discovery 56
Chapter 9 Choosing a Life of Clarity and Strength 74
Chapter 10 The Final Step: Embracing the Gift of Now 84

About the Author

Samantha Holsomback is the owner of All Things Love-Event Planning. She is a veteran creator and manager for event logistics, has served many notable businesses in and around her city since 2015, and has been recognized as one of the Top 100 Influential Women in her community. Other accolades include being a published author featured in part of the anthologies, including the Amazon bestseller, "YOU CAN," and a second book entitled, "STRONGER." She has been awarded Rotarian of the Year, is a Community Advisor for The Task Force Against Human Trafficking, and she is a co-host on Find Her Seat Podcast. Samantha was a showcased Runway Model for 2024 and 2025 New York Fashion Week, and is a married mother of two children who enjoys fashion, music, traveling, and supporting philanthropic organizations that advocate for her community.

Page Blank Intentionally

Chapter 1
The Ripple Effect

Everything changes when you stop drinking. It might seem like a simple statement, but trust me, it's more than just a catchy phrase; to me, it's the very foundation of a transformative journey that redefined my entire life. I remember the chaotic days when my decisions impacted everyone I loved. My mind was a whirlwind of noise, thoughts spiraling out of control, leaving little room for clarity. I would make late-night phone calls, uncertain of the reason behind them, my voice louder and more unsure than it should have been. I disturbed friends and family in their slumber, asking them questions about everything in the world. Conversations became a blur as moments were lost to the fog of alcohol. I'd nod along, only to forget critical details the next day, leaving me feeling disconnected and ashamed. That phase of my life will haunt me forever.

The result of those nights was always the same: I'd wake up in a cold sweat, my body would ache, I would have a pounding headache that would feel almost fatal, and worst of all, nausea that just wouldn't go for hours. I would no longer be in a physical and mental state to interact with anyone and, hence, would avoid phone calls and messages, withdrawing into isolation and waiting for the hours to pass. It was a miserable cycle, one that drained my energy and stripped away my confidence. In the hours that followed my drinking session, I craved junk food to crush the hangover while simultaneously battling a low-grade fever. The only thing I felt confident of was that this life was not what I wanted, yet I felt powerless to change it. However, as I decided to step away from alcohol, something extraordinary began to happen. I gradually noticed that the fog that had clouded my mind for so long finally started to lift, and my ability to handle high-stress situations improved dramatically. I cared less about trivial matters, letting go of concerns that once consumed my thoughts and stressed me beyond what I could bear. I became more discerning with my time and energy, no longer willing to tolerate things that wasted them. And for the first time in my life, after a very long time, I was able to view everything optimistically. I knew that a bright future awaited me, and I couldn't wait to get there. This newfound clarity was intoxicating in its own way.

This was a completely new space for me, and in this space, I began to reevaluate my life and how I valued myself and others. My self-worth once depended on social validation, but now, it has transformed into something deeper and more authentic. I learned to cherish genuine connections and prioritize relationships, be they friendships or family, that nurtured me rather than those that drained me physically and spiritually. Unfortunately, some relationships naturally fell apart, probably because they weren't formed with the real me but with the version of me that I became after I consumed alcohol. Surprisingly, most grew deeper and more meaningful. I became dependable and trustworthy— qualities I had long neglected. I also gained support I thought I never had, and that's when I realized I wasn't alone. The friends who remained in my life became my support system and guiding force. They celebrated my victories, as small as they were, and listened to my dreams and believed in them. There were countless times when I doubted myself and thought of returning to the old ways, but these people constantly reminded me why I had embarked on this journey in the first place. Our conversations shifted from idle gossip to deep discussions about our aspirations, fears, and struggles. I found comfort in these honest interactions, celebrating the authenticity of genuine connections that mattered. It was as if a weight had been lifted, allowing me to breathe freely for the first time in years.

It wasn't just my personal life that changed; my professional life flourished, too. I had always worked hard, having been working since I was 15, sometimes juggling two jobs at a time. So, I was no stranger to hard work, but when I started drinking, opportunities began slipping from my hands even when I knew I was qualified and capable of grabbing them. When I finally decided to get sober, it rekindled my ambition. With a clear mind, I rediscovered my drive and began chasing prospects I had previously overlooked. My work ethic grew, and the quality of my work got better than it ever was. I found myself booking more jobs than ever before as I was returning emails promptly, something I hadn't done in quite a while.

I had owned an event planning firm for nearly a decade, but in the past, alcohol had affected my potential. For a very long time, I had been circling, hesitant to pursue new gigs because my doubt stopped me and left my growth stunned. But now, with sobriety, I reevaluated my passions and solidified contracts with newfound confidence. The bookings became consistent, and I could feel the momentum building. I could sense that my life was changing, and I was ready for what it had in store. With each day, I became proud of who I was becoming and finally let go of the regret, anxiety, and depression that had been a part of me for a long time. My sleep improved dramatically; I no longer woke up in a haze of guilt and nausea. Instead, as I got up every morning, I was greeted by the clarity of morning light. I was ready to seize the day! I also began to embrace healthier eating habits, powering my body with nourishment rather than junk food. My physical appearance transformed alongside my mental state. Unlike before, I now had clear thoughts because I was no longer sick and constantly exhausted. Most importantly, this newfound energy made me even more productive.

I've always had a passion for fashion. It is something that I have wanted to pursue and work toward but didn't find the courage to do so. However, little did I know that my sobriety would eventually lead me toward my dream. The pinnacle of my transformation was when I received an invitation to walk the runway for New York Fashion Week—not just for 2024, but for 2025. It felt surreal. Doing so had been a dream for so long, and now it was finally coming to life. I rejoiced in the glory of these experiences. I knew it was all happening because I had chosen to change my life. Each moment spent preparing for the runway felt like evidence that your life, no matter how it feels in the moment, eventually comes together; you have to believe in yourself.

With positive experiences in my personal and professional life, I learned to set goals and work toward them without the added pressure of unrealistic expectations. I knew that success was a possibility that I should aim for, but it was no longer the only thing I was hoping for. Instead, now I hoped for better experiences and more learning opportunities. The anxiety and depression that had once shadowed my entire life now began to scatter. They were replaced by a calm assurance that I was on the right path, and even though the path was long, I knew I would eventually get to where I aimed for. Yet, what hurt me the most during this time was that not everyone understood my journey. I faced criticism from some who believed my sobriety was just a phase and that I would eventually go back to drinking and making the same old choices. It was sometimes disheartening, but I learned to embrace the haters and their doubts as part of my growth. Their disbelief fueled my fire, pushing me to prove to them and myself that I could thrive in this new chapter of my life.

Sitting with my pen in hand, I realized this chapter was just the beginning. My journey of sobriety is an ongoing one, but it has brought me to a place of empowerment, clarity, and purpose that I hope continues for the rest of my life. I embrace the changes that have come and the growth that continues to unfold. Each day is evidence of my resilience and determination to live a life full of intention and authenticity. In fact, it wouldn't be wrong if I said that every step I took in my aim to get rid of alcohol created a ripple effect in my life that ultimately led to where I am today. Today, I see the world as an empty canvas waiting for me to fill it with opportunities and experiences that come my way. The journey ahead is bright, and I am ready to embrace it with both arms open. I hope that whoever reads this, if they are struggling with the same problems I have struggled with, gets the courage to start their life all over again. I hope they realize that no matter what has happened in the past, life is still very much worth living.

Chapter 2
Embracing Your Inner Evolution

I have seen people hold themselves back when they feel they're changing. They are too afraid of the new adventures coming their way, frightened of the uncertainty of life and what it brings, causing them to stay stagnant forever. I genuinely believe that we humans are not meant to be stagnant; we are born to grow, evolve, and uplift one another. Sure, we all make mistakes, but rather than seeing them as things that should hold us back, we must consider them as parts of the journey and confront them to change negative patterns. Often, we cling to what we believe is good, not realizing we're grasping at the remains of something that once served us but no longer does.

I have been on a similar journey: a journey of making mistakes and eventually learning from them, a journey of realizing the negative patterns and letting them go, and a journey that, no matter how tough, ended up serving the greater good. I speak from personal experience when I say that it takes tremendous courage to confront the errors you make in life, to dig deep, and to change the negative patterns that have shaped us. However, this transformation is not just a possibility; it is a necessity for true fulfillment.

It is easy to romanticize the past, to think of all the good things that happened, and forget about the bad ones. We think of our past as a sanctuary, a place much more familiar and too comfortable, when, in reality, it may be a prison of our own making. It is a universal experience that makes so many of us find ourselves addicted to the very things that were once our solace. To me, it was alcohol. The numbness that came with alcohol shielded me from feeling all the uncomfortable emotions that I desperately tried to avoid. As isolated and withdrawn as I felt afterward, the moment when my first drink touched my lips, I would feel elevated, as if all my worries had disappeared. The lightness I felt in that moment came to haunt me the very next day as the world came shattering down on me, making me regret every decision I had taken the night before. Unfortunately, I still wouldn't stop. It was a loop, and I was stuck badly.

To this day, whenever I remember that time, I feel a certain void left by something familiar, but that's when I remind myself of the life-sucking loop I was stuck in. I know it can be hard to recognize this loop while you're stuck in it, but remember, that's when you need to ask for help and embrace the change that comes with it.

Samantha Holsomback

In fact, when you look around, change is something you would see in everything. Nature is the biggest endorser of change. Every organism around us has shown change, perhaps because change and evolution are the only constants in this life. Take the butterfly, for example, a splendid symbol of transformation. It emerges from the confines of its cocoon, rising through the sky without a look back at its former self, the caterpillar. This natural metamorphosis teaches us an important lesson: our evolution and the importance of embracing our past without shame because when you do that, you become your most powerful self. Just like the butterfly, when you shed what no longer serves you, you welcome what truly helps; it is both beautiful and necessary. The caterpillar does not mourn its previous form; instead, it celebrates its new reality, a reminder that growth often comes with discomfort.

I, too, went through a familiar journey of transformation when I quit alcohol. I remember a time when panic was the center of my life, clouding my thoughts and suffocating my soul. Each day felt like a battle against an unseen force, a force so strong that it could consume me whole. I constantly wrestled with anxiety and self-doubt, devaluing myself, my potential, and my will to carry on in life. It was a chaotic phase, but it was also the time when my strength was stimulated.

Slowly, through self analyzation and determination, I began to shift my focus from what was wrong to what could be right. I went from feeling panicky all the time to finally being at peace and content with my life and what it had for me in store. I discovered that my health and self-worth are non-negotiable, and anyone or anything that makes me compromise with these needs to go away. The moment I grasped this truth, everything began to change. I stopped allowing external validation to dictate my feelings and started recognizing the value within myself. I learned that the foundation of true happiness must be built from within, not being dependent on others or the circumstances surrounding me.

The truth is, it wasn't easy, none of it was. Embracing the change that comes from within is frightening, and yes, it scared me, too. For as long as I can remember, I have always been someone who has compromised on various aspects of my life, trying to please those around me, despite how unhappy it made me in the long run. But now, I wanted to embrace the change that I felt from within. Embracing my struggles became a transformative practice. I realized that every moment of hardship was an opportunity for growth. I no longer felt embarrassed by my journey; instead, I celebrated it. Each setback, each painful experience, became a stepping stone toward becoming the person I had always aspired to be. I began to see my struggles as badges of honor that proved my resilience and commitment to my own evolution.

I realized that what had stopped me from embracing change all these years was my constant need to control my life and everything around me. Letting go of old habits felt like I was stepping onto a path explored, and that made me anxious more than anything. In the beginning, surrender felt like weakness, a defeat to the chaos surrounding me, a chaos I was unfamiliar with. I needed to let go of my obsession to control every aspect of my life and allow the currents of life to guide me rather than constantly fighting against them. And in this state of surrender, I became an alchemist, changing my pain into beauty.

I often compare my life's transformation to alchemy because I think it fits perfectly. I wasn't always very fond of it, but with each challenge I faced, I began to understand the concept of alchemy in a deeper, more profound sense. Alchemy is often associated with the mystical transformation of base metals into gold, but for me, its true essence lies in the ability to transform the ordinary into the extraordinary. My evolution has allowed me to take the heavy burdens of my past, like the guilt, the shame, and the fear, and transform them into strength and light. It took me a while, but I made what once held me back into the fuel that ultimately helped my growth. I started practicing gratitude as an everyday ritual. Each day, I took a moment to reflect on the lessons learned from my struggles, allowing me to shift my perspective. Instead of viewing challenges as obstacles, I began to see them as teachers. This shift not only lightened my heart but also my journey through life ahead. I became aware of all the countless ways life was inviting me to grow, and I embraced each lesson with open arms because now nothing was holding me back, not alcohol, not my fears, nothing!

This newfound change also transformed the way I viewed relationships. I became more empathetic and understanding of the struggles faced by others. I recognized that everyone has their own battles that are often hidden beneath the surface. Just like I have struggled in the past, many people around me have too. This awareness deepened my connections with those around me, fostering a sense of shared experience. And like I mentioned earlier, we humans are meant to help one another along the way, and so I did. Remember, help doesn't always have to be tangible; sometimes, the biggest help you can give someone is by being there for them. I know this because when I was on my transformative journey, the presence of my friends and family was the one thing that kept me going. For this, you need not be afraid of being vulnerable, for your strength lies in vulnerability. I know that sharing your experiences can be daunting, especially when you have outgrown them and don't want people to see you in the same light, but trust me, when you open up, you realize that so many around you resonate with your story because they have had similar experiences. How will you ever connect with these people if you do not give yourself a chance to be vulnerable?

As I look back at my journey of self-evolution, I see struggles and triumphs, but most importantly, I see lessons that I learned along the way. Today, I'm proud to admit that I no longer see my past as a matter of shame or regret; rather, I see it as an integral part of the person I am today. The good, the bad, the ugly, I embrace all of it with open arms. By sharing my story, I hope to inspire others to embark on their own journeys of embracing change and becoming the person they are meant to be. We all possess the ability to transform our pain into light, to turn our struggles into sources of strength. It's true that no one is exempt from hardship; it is part of the human experience, but how we respond to these challenges shapes our destiny.

Chapter 3
The Devil is a Glass of Wine

In each of our lives, there is a devil. It could be a person, someone close to us, or even a stranger who makes us doubt ourselves, a thing, an addiction, a habit, or sometimes our own internal battles. These devils, whether external or internal, form a web of challenges that hinder our growth and potential until we take accountability for them and try to overcome them. You have to choose to break free from these destructive devils, take control of your destiny, and set forth a path of genuine progress. In my life, this devil came in a glass; it came to kill, steal, and destroy me.

For years, I'd believed the lie that alcohol amplified my spirit. When I was drunk, I thought I became the life of the party, the one who could make even the dullest moments and gatherings feel vibrant. But what I mistook for fun had transformed into something ugly. I had become obnoxious, a caricature of the person I aspired to be. I could still hear the whispers of people, their laughter mixed with concern, but the truth lay heavy beneath the surface, and only I knew that, even if I didn't want to admit it at the moment. With each drink, I slipped further away from my true self. The charm I thought I was projecting morphed into harshness, and the delightful banter turned into clumsy attempts at humor. On one end, where I felt that my personality was shining brighter than ever, the shadows that alcohol cast grew. It was a paradox that left me feeling isolated amidst the thrumming crowd.

The truth is that alcohol felt like a familiar companion. I was with it for far too long, and hence, I became too comfortable with it. I had a hard time recognizing all the harm it was causing me. However, despite the challenges, taking accountability became essential at one point. I had come to realize that alcohol had brought a series of adverse effects into my life— impairing my judgment, diminishing my self-worth, and stripping away my authentic self. Each drink was a step further into a mist that clouded my vision, hindering my goals and ambitions. I used to think of alcohol as a social lubricant, but now it had become a chain that bound me, pulling me down into behaviors and patterns I no longer wanted to accept.

Unlike what I thought, I was no longer the life of the party; I wasn't fun anymore. I was just a woman so innately dependent on her glass of wine that without it, everything felt incomplete— a total blur. That's when I knew I had to change my ways. I could no longer allow alcohol to dictate my life; I had to evolve and elevate. It was going to be the biggest decision of my life, one that would change its trajectory forever, but I was in desperate need of change, and that's how my journey to sobriety started.

As I embraced the commitment to remain sober, I was filled with confidence and excitement about the benefits that awaited me. I believed that my life would change completely, and I couldn't wait for it to happen. The choice I made was difficult, but it wasn't just about abstaining from alcohol; it was also about reclaiming my life and nurturing my true self. I had lost far too many experiences due to the haze of alcohol, and I was not going to let that happen anymore. What motivated me the most was the fact that I wasn't in it alone; I knew that being addicted to the highs that alcohol gives you was a serious problem, and millions of people around the world dealt with it. It causes numerous health problems and legal issues, affected families, and was linked to academic and professional failures. It made me upset just thinking about how destructive it can be, and yet so many people, just like me, have such a hard time quitting it.

I once read somewhere that alcohol consumption causes around 2.6 million deaths around the world. It plays a significant role in injuries, aggression, and violence, and many of these affect society in ways we can't even imagine. The truth is that alcohol goes beyond one's self and well-being; it is a slippery slope and has adverse economic and societal costs. Despite knowing how harmful alcohol can be, many of us make the conscious decision to indulge in it, mainly because eliminating it from our lives can be so difficult. You look around you, and you see people still enjoying a glass of wine, the same glass that was your biggest enemy, and, in that moment, it is so hard to control yourself. What you need to understand is that the change you're looking for needs to come from within you, and when that happens, you will not care about what is around you.

One of the most significant shifts I've made in this journey is my approach to social gatherings. I recognize that these events will continue to exist, and alcohol will likely be present in them. I can't avoid all of them, in fact, I don't want to. I can't let alcohol dictate my life in any way, which is why I will still attend these occasions and even arrange work events that involve alcohol. However, my relationship with these environments will be entirely different. I will remain committed to my decision, focusing on the connections I can foster without the influence of alcohol clouding my judgment. I refuse to let the presence of alcohol dictate my enjoyment or my ability to engage fully with others.

I try to find comfort in the idea that my journey toward sobriety is not a solitary one. Many people are on similar paths, seeking to break free from the curse of alcohol. Sharing experiences with others who understand the challenges can be empowering. I envision myself engaging with others in these social situations, finding common ground in our shared goals of clarity and authenticity. This newfound perspective allows me to see social gatherings not as traps but as opportunities to practice my commitment to sobriety while still enjoying the company of friends. I believe I must stay aware of the underlying motivation behind my old drinking habits. For many years, I used alcohol to cope with crippling anxiety and social pressure. I assumed that a drink would loosen me up and that it would make mingling easier and conversations flow more freely. However, looking back, I can see how waves of regret and embarrassment often followed those moments of apparent ease. The confidence I wanted from a drink ultimately led to feelings of inadequacy and self-loathing later. So, when I embarked on my sobriety journey, my biggest battle wasn't with alcohol itself but rather with the uncomforting feeling that I tried to mask with it. This means I had to learn to sit with my discomfort, acknowledge my feelings, and understand that vulnerability is not a weakness. I kept telling myself that it's part of human nature. Each moment of discomfort is an opportunity for growth, and I want to lean into that discomfort rather than run from it.

As I move forward, I am acutely focused on the benefits I will achieve. I envision clearer conversations, authentic connections, and moments of joy that are not followed by regret. I know that I have a fun personality without alcohol, and although I have used alcohol to amplify it, I am just as equally lively and fun without it. However, today, my definition of fun is much different from what it used to be. I once believed that fun was synonymous with drinking, but I now see that joy can be found in many experiences. Whether it's exploring a new hobby, taking a spontaneous trip with friends, or simply enjoying a quiet evening with a book, I can cultivate joy in ways that are sustainable and fulfilling. This shift in mindset opens up a world of possibilities, allowing me to explore life without the limitations that alcohol imposes.

Today, each social interaction is an opportunity to shine as my true self, unhindered by the fog of alcohol. I imagine myself at parties, engaging in laughter and meaningful discussions, feeling fully present and alive in each moment. And trust me, it's not as easy as it sounds. Challenges come my way all the time, and I know many more lie ahead. There will be many moments of temptation, and there will be days when I feel low. It's easy to think that one drink wouldn't hurt, that I could handle it, that I could still have fun. However, now that I have this newfound clarity, I am able to make wiser choices. I know that one drink can spiral into many drinks and days of hangover and ultimately going back to the place I have been running from.

This journey is about transformation—about evolving into a version of myself that thrives rather than barely survives. I want to take accountability for my choices and actions, recognizing that they shape the person I am becoming. The decision to remain sober has also encouraged me to take a closer look at my health and well-being. I've begun to prioritize physical fitness, finding joy in moving my body and keeping it active. This shift not only improves my physical health but also positively impacts my mental well-being. Trust me, the endorphins produced doing this are incomparable to when I consumed alcohol.

To most people, I might just be walking away from alcohol, but to me, it is so much more than that. I am stepping into a life filled with potential, purpose, and authenticity, something that alcohol has kept me away from. I want to embrace each day as an opportunity to build a brighter future, one where I am free from the chains of my past.

With every passing day, I feel more empowered to live my truth. I am learning to celebrate my victories, acknowledge the progress I've made, and embrace the journey ahead with open arms. My life is no longer defined by the devil in the glass; instead, it is shaped by the choices I make and the relationships I nurture. I am excited about the journey ahead, filled with promise and the prospect of rediscovering who I truly am—unfiltered and unapologetically me.

Chapter 4
From Cheers to Tears

Rock bottom means different things to different people. For some, it's the gut-wrenching moment of losing a job, a relationship, or even a sense of self. For me, it wasn't something that happened all of a sudden; instead, it was a gradual descent—a series of choices that spiraled into a lifestyle defined by a lack of ambition and little concern for myself or others. Each time I hit what I thought was rock bottom, I simply redefined the term, allowing it to shift like sand beneath my feet. Ultimately, rock bottom became a moving line, blurring the boundaries of my reality, with consequences piling up like laundry in the corner of a messy room.

My journey began innocently enough, a glass of wine here, a beer there. Social events turned into late-night adventures, and what was once an occasional indulgence transformed into a ritualistic practice. I justified each drink, convinced that it helped me feel relaxed, loosen up, be more open, and connect with my friends. Yet, as my consumption grew, so did the side effects. It was soon that I started noticing an expanding waistline, low energy, and a complexion that lacked the vibrancy of youth. The physical symptoms were easy to ignore, but the emotional toll was worse—my thoughts were always clouded by a creeping fog that not only made me hazy but also dimmed my motivation. Endless sad thoughts floated through my mind, and my memories became blurred like a watercolor painting that was left in rain. I didn't know what was going on with me, but whatever it was, it didn't feel right.

I had begun to see the difference between the new me and the one I had left behind, and it scared me. Some days, I wouldn't even recognize myself, and that was when I knew it was time to change. Then came the day when everything clicked. I stood before the mirror, staring at the reflection of someone I hardly recognized. I knew I was only hurting myself, my future, and those around me. The realization hit me like a punch to the gut: I no longer wanted to feel this way. I was tired, so tired! Alcohol was not serving me; it was shackling me. I was caught up in a cycle of regret, shame, and self-sabotage for far too long, but now, after a really long time, a flicker of hope kindled within me. Something from within said that I could change this.

Educating myself was the first step. I read books and articles about sobriety and healthy living. I discovered tactics that would help me jump into this vast, frightening part of life that existed without alcohol. I framed out a tailored set of cognitive commitments, a promise to myself that I would uphold. Obviously, avoiding alcohol was the first thing on that list, but that wasn't it; I needed a plan to navigate this new territory.

The first thing I did was commit to avoiding places where people went solely to consume alcohol. I drew a line: Bars were out, at least for now. I set a routine of going to bed at a regular time, something I hadn't done in years. I started eating better, organizing my space, and taking time out for workouts. Reading became an escape, a way to nourish my mind and spirit. I poured my energy into my career, striving for excellence in my work, and pursued cultivating deeper connections with loved ones through activities that didn't revolve around drinking.

The truth is, I knew that alcohol wasn't my addiction; I was addicted to the habitual practices that dictated my decision-making. I had started believing that drinking alcohol was the norm, and sadly, the belief that I needed to drink to socialize was like a mental block, a chain that had wrapped around me for far too long. If I was in a social setting, alcohol felt like a requirement. Bad day? Pour some drink and call it a day. Good day? Time to celebrate and drink even harder. In my mind, being lively and fun required alcohol, but the truth was, I had been sleeping with the enemy. Each drink blurred my memories and dulled my emotions, leading to regrets that piled over one another.

I had hit rock bottom more times than I cared to admit, each time thinking, "This can't get worse." But I was wrong; it got worse, so much worse. The anvil of regret weighed heavy on me—each careless word, each thoughtless action echoed in my mind, and I found myself on my knees, begging for relief. I no longer wanted to hurt myself or those I loved. However, changing things wasn't as easy as I thought. The uncertainty of the unknown felt scary. It was unthinkable to imagine a life free of alcohol, a life where I could still connect with friends and celebrate milestones without the safety net of a drink in hand. However, I began to understand that just because something was difficult didn't mean it was impossible. And so, I decided to be brave and venture into this unfamiliar territory with hopes to change my life forever.

I focused on reframing my relationships. The friendships that thrived only over cocktails weakened when I stopped drinking, but in their place, I formed new connections—relationships built on truth, shared interests, and genuine care. I had been so wrapped up in the idea that drinking was essential to friendship that I hadn't recognized the joy of connecting with people sober and getting to know who they really were. I learned to embrace activities that didn't revolve around alcohol, and I found joy in laughter that didn't stem from a drink and in conversations that were clearer and more meaningful.

As I began to prioritize my health, I noticed a shift within me. I had spent years neglecting my physical well-being, but the more I exercised and ate healthily, the more lively I felt. My energy increased, and my mood lifted, leaving little room for despair and self-doubt.

I discovered that I could still have fun without the fog of alcohol. Celebrating milestones became more profound. I learned to savor moments—like the morning run or the sound of laughter shared over coffee. As I changed my perspective on joy, I realized that alcohol had never truly enhanced my life; it had only masked my insecurities and fears while giving me crippling anxiety, creating a cycle of unproductivity and self-disrespect. I had created a new level of rock bottom each time, but that had to stop. I had to break the chains of my limiting beliefs and create a shift.

I fully accepted that in order to have a real change, I have to focus on what truly requires my energy and attention. Instead of seeing alcohol as a friend, I had to view it as what it truly was: an enemy with the intent to dismantle the good relationships I had with my children, my family, my friends, my career, and even my finances.

No matter how difficult it was, I had to admit that it was taking advantage of my vulnerabilities. I had to finally shut the door.

It was liberating to let go of the influences that had kept me trapped. I accepted the real change required, which was learning to let go—sometimes people, sometimes places, and often old habits. To do that, I surrounded myself with peers who supported my newfound lifestyle and shared my values. I shifted my focus from what I had lost to the improvement in my quality of life, the relationships that nourished my soul, and the sense of self-love that blossomed within me. In this journey of rediscovery, I came to understand that I had the power to reshape my narrative, even if the cheers have turned into tears. I was living proof that change while challenging, was entirely attainable. My friendships and family life flourished in ways I had never anticipated, and I finally felt free from the shackles of my past.

Most of all, my rock bottom has finally shifted, revealing a foundation built on self-awareness, strength, and resilience. I am no longer afraid of bitter truths and confrontations, running from my true self, but instead, now I run toward a brighter future. I have chosen a path that aligns with my values, a life where health has truly become my wealth. Each day, I wake up with clarity, ready to embrace the world with open arms and a heart full of gratitude.

As I look ahead, I understand that life will always present challenges. But now, armed with the lessons of my past and a newfound sense of purpose, I am ready to face them head-on. I have chosen to live, to thrive, and to celebrate life—not in a glass, but in every moment I am fully present. And there is nothing that compares to it because it is the most beautiful gift of all.

Chapter 5
Beyond the Glamour

It's almost baffling how the world media has created a sensation around alcohol, so much so that today, it appeals to people of all ages. From the glitzy commercials flashing across our screens to the social media posts about night outs with friends, the media's portrayal of alcohol is alarming. However, the worst part is that no one really sees it like that; instead, media sensationalism has forced people to see alcohol consumption as a melody with laughter, adventure, and the promise of good times. Yet, amidst this intoxicating narrative, I often find myself pondering a crucial question: why does society devote countless resources to commercials about the dangers of cigarettes and drugs while the hazardous effects of alcohol remain covered in a veil of celebration?

Today, society has become so used to celebrating every happiness, every achievement, even the smallest joys and setbacks with alcohol that it is no longer looked at as harmful. This normalization has led to a lot of alcohol advertisements being targeted at young people, encouraging them to have a can of beer to relax and have a good time. This is a confusing reality, especially for someone like me, who has dealt with the bittersweet aftermath of drinking. I've been in a position where I thought a glass or two wouldn't hurt, especially because it was normalized, but it didn't take long for me to realize that I was headed to the path of destruction.

I remember vividly the early days of my sobriety when the weight of depression felt heavy on my chest. It wasn't a sorrowful kind of depression but rather a momentary pause—a much-needed rest from the chaotic identity I had made for myself. I was a mother, a wife, a worker, and a friend, each role demanding a version of me that often felt compromised by the haze of alcohol. However, stepping away from that fog was not just about quitting the old lifestyle; it was about embracing the opportunity to rest, reflect, and ultimately reconfigure my life.

In those first weeks of sobriety, the emotions were raw and unsettling. I found myself navigating through the leftovers of my past—shame, guilt, and ever-present flashbacks to moments I wished I could forget. Memories of embarrassing times and foolish decisions haunted me, a relentless reminder of how alcohol had distorted my life's narrative. Yet, in this sadness, I recognized a fundamental truth: This low, just like the high from drinking, was temporary.

My brain, much like a toddler deprived of candy,

threw tantrums as I withdrew from its usual indulgences. It had gotten so used to being constantly in a fog that now that it was clear, it felt strange. My brain cried out for the sweet, numbing relief that alcohol once provided, but I had to remember that indulging this desire would not serve my well-being. I had been depriving myself of the basic ingredients that sustain a healthy mind and body, and it was no surprise that my withdrawal brought forth sadness. I was simply healing—a process that required patience and compassion for myself.

I would wake up without the familiar jabbing headache or the uncertainty of where I had stumbled the night before, and it felt like stepping into a new life. I no longer had to wince at the sight of questionable bruises or cringe while reading through the shambles of drunken text exchanges. I didn't have to relive the ridiculous snapshots of myself taken the night before and feel embarrassed looking at them. Instead, I greeted each morning with a clarity that I had lost for so long. However, this newfound clarity came at a cost.

The first few weeks were filled with fatigue and confusion as my body struggled to recalibrate after years of overindulgence. I initially thought that if I started making the right choices, my body would instantly respond in a positive way and reward me, but little did I know that things did not work that easily because, biologically, it was impossible.

I learned that my body was working overtime, repairing itself from the internal chaos I had inflicted over time. The initial fatigue was not a punishment but a necessary phase of restoration to my old self. So, I chose to retreat from the activities that once filled my calendar. Outside of caring for my children and attending to work and chores, I took out moments of rest. Rest for me was sleeping, reading my favorite books, taking long baths, going on walks with my sweet Yorkie pup, working out, cleaning my wardrobe, and enjoying quality time with my husband and kids.

Slowly but surely, the chaos of my life began to transform. As I focused on healing, my home became a sanctuary of order and tranquility. I felt revitalized, and the elevated stress levels that once shadowed my life as dark clouds vanished. I felt revitalized and almost like a new person, a person I could proudly look in the mirror without the overwhelming shame and guilt. The changes I saw and felt in myself were also reflected around me. The atmosphere at home dramatically changed, becoming peaceful, a stark contrast to the intense years of drinking. I began to rediscover who I was, shedding the layers of a false identity that alcohol had created.

One major step I had to take was to get back out there and start attending the social gatherings I was always a vibrant part of. Like I've said before, I couldn't let alcohol stop me from being the person I was. So, I cautiously approached the idea of re-entering social settings. I took baby steps, selecting outings that felt safe and supportive. Over time, the anxiety that once gripped me in social situations began to significantly lessen. I learned to enjoy gatherings without the help of alcohol, navigating these experiences with newfound confidence. Each outing became a stepping stone, a day-by-day journey of rebuilding my social life without the haze of drinking.

Surrendering to these changes and embracing a new way of living was revolutionary. Reflecting on my transformation, I recognized that I was not the same person I had been a year ago. I had outgrown certain relationships and left behind familiar environments, but rather than crying over these losses, I felt a profound sense of peace. God had been guiding me through a journey I hadn't even known I needed so much, steering me toward the life I had always desired. Now, I had to trust the process, for it was the most important step. I entered into a new season of my life—one with purpose and growth.

While I still faced challenges, I no longer felt the pressure of giving up. Too much was at stake, and I could see the direct correlation between my discipline and my successes. I was born with a relentless drive—a refusal to be average—and it became my greatest asset in this journey toward self-discovery.

Striving to be a better person, not just for myself but for others, became paramount. I was able to show up as my highest self—fully and unapologetically— and there was no greater gift than that. The ugly parts of my story became a powerful testimony, a story of resilience that I now carry with pride.

Today, I wake up to a fresh face, unburdened by bloating or memory loss. I face each day head-on, free of regret, together with the ability to go anywhere without the shadow of a hangover. Each morning, I remind myself of the incredible strength I've found in this journey—strength that was rooted in vulnerability and thirst to make a better life for myself.

In this new chapter of my life, I've learned to embrace joy without the need for artificial highs. I've finally discovered a connection to my authentic self, one that flourishes in the absence of substances like alcohol. The laughter that now fills my home is genuine, echoing from authenticity rather than a fleeting sense of high experience after alcohol.

Samantha Holsomback

My journey of sobriety has not just reshaped my relationship with alcohol but has also strengthened my connections with family and friends. I no longer rush moments as I've come to appreciate the beauty in shared moments that require nothing more than being present and authentic. I've learned to be fully engaged in the lives of those I love, unbothered by external distractions like intoxication. I am continuously evolving, learning to navigate the complexities of life. The pull of alcohol may still be present somewhere in the background, but it no longer holds power over me; I no longer get pulled. Instead, I find solace in the quiet moments, the simple joys of everyday life—moments that remind me of how important the journey of sobriety is and why I embarked on it.

Today, I recognize that the media's portrayal of alcohol can be misleading, glamorizing a lifestyle that often leads to chaos and pain in the end. While the world may revel in the idea of drinking as a source of joy, I stand as a witness to the beauty of embracing life without it. Each day, I celebrate the victories—both big and small—that have come from my commitment to sobriety.

Chapter 6
Embracing A New Life Without Alcohol

It's true; when you leave alcohol, your entire life changes. For most people, alcohol isn't just a beverage they enjoy from time to time; it rather becomes that one thing their entire life revolves around. When you sleep and wake up, who you hang out with, where you spend your leisure time, how much time you give your family, how much effort you put into your work, how your mental health functions, basically everything becomes reliant on alcohol. Hence, quitting becomes a lifestyle change, one that needs your entire dedication and effort beyond what you could have ever imagined.

When I decided to let go of alcohol, I wasn't just saying goodbye to a drink in a glass. I was severing ties with a lifestyle, with a host of in-built habits, and ultimately with a part of myself that I had leaned on—sometimes heavily—for years. I've got to admit, moving away from a life that often revolved around bars, parties, and "just one more drink" has been both freeing and frightening. I'm choosing to become a new person, yet this journey has unveiled how challenging it is to redefine myself without the numbness and social support that alcohol provides.

In the beginning, I thought the hardest part would be saying "no" to the drink. However, I quickly realized that resisting a drink was just the tip of the iceberg. Beneath that act was a complex experience: Learning to sit with emotions I'd numbed for so long, redefining how I relate to friends and family, and even relearning how to relax and have fun. Finding hobbies that don't involve drinking has felt like stepping into a new world—a world that's not foggy and muted but alive with complex intricacies and edges I had forgotten existed.

Every day is a mix of emotions. I experience both highs and lows depending on the day. There are mornings when I wake up feeling proud, strong, and empowered, as though I can take on anything. Then there are afternoons when the reality sets in, and it feels like a heavy weight I carry alone. The isolation is unexpectedly confusing. I used to fit in so easily at social gatherings, sliding seamlessly into conversations and laughter, even with strangers. The glass of wine in my hand seemed to keep all anxiety and self-consciousness at bay.

But now, without it, I sometimes feel like I don't quite know who I am and what I am doing, surrounded by all these people I didn't resonate with. In these sober moments, I'm often forced to confront a version of myself that feels raw and incomplete. I look around at others and wonder if they notice this version of me that I'm still getting used to.

At times, there's an overwhelming rush of euphoria, a deep sense of joy and empowerment that comes with this decision. I feel incredible to have broken free from a cycle that had held me captive. Unfortunately, the euphoria is often followed by the realization of how much work there is still to do and how many challenging days might lie ahead. The moments of joy are real, but so are the waves of frustration, tears, and confusion that come crashing in, reminding me that this isn't a simple journey. It's a constant balancing act between feeling proud of how far I've come and managing realistic expectations.

I so badly want to be the best version of myself, not just for me but for my children, my family, and my marriage. I know that my relationship with alcohol was standing in the way of that future. It wasn't an addiction in the usual sense, but it was something that I struggled to control, something that too often left me feeling like I wasn't fully present in my own life, being unable to make important decisions.

The truth is, alcohol blurred the edges of how I felt,

thought, and operated—not always, but often enough that it became a problem. And it's haunting how something that was supposed to bring joy and relaxation instead became this invisible chain around my life. I guess there's a reason they call it "spirits"; even when the night is over, alcohol leaves a trace, remaining in the body and mind like a ghost. Planning my day after a night of drinking became tough in its own way—preparing for the hand tremors, the waves of sweat, the uncontrollable cravings, the desperate need for sleep, the constant headache that wouldn't subside. My heart breaks now that I think of all the experiences I missed out on because I was scared of how my body was reacting and because I couldn't fully be there. I lost so many moments to drinking, not always because I wanted to but because I felt trapped in a cycle I couldn't break. I'd tell myself over and over that I'd just have one drink, that I wouldn't take shots or stay out too late, but deep down, I knew those were just words; I wasn't strong enough to keep those promises.

Girls' nights turned into mornings, date nights became binge sessions, and weekends bled into difficult Mondays.

My fuel to drink, despite how awful it made me feel afterward, was my stubbornness. I've always believed that stubbornness was my greatest weakness, but little did I know that it was also my greatest strength. It is my stubborn nature that has sustained me in this journey toward sobriety. When I finally made the decision to stop, I tapped into that same stubbornness, telling myself that nothing could get in the way of this change. I've lost close friends to this lifestyle, and I began to see that the path I was on could lead me to join them really soon. This thought was sobering in more ways than one, and I knew I had to pull myself away from that road before it was too late.

The first year was the roughest; there were endless challenges that tested my determination. Life didn't slow down to give me time to process my choice. I had to face the worsening condition of my grandmother, whose dementia had stolen her memories of me. I was betrayed by a friend in a way that cut deeply. Old acquaintances watched me with curiosity as my lifestyle changed, some even with a hint of doubt as if waiting for me to stumble so they could prove a 'point.' And then there were the triggers—the concerts, the vacations, the social gatherings where everyone else had a drink in hand.

At first, it was difficult to resist alcohol, especially in those moments when it seemed like it would make things easier, perhaps more fun. But over time, I started to feel a new kind of strength growing within me, and what once felt impossible slowly became manageable. Today, most of these triggers have started to fade, like ghosts; I can now see through them instead of being haunted by them.

Choosing sobriety has meant redefining what it means to cope, what it means to celebrate, and what it means to unwind. Earlier, I had let myself be a victim of my own choices, constantly caught in a cycle that I convinced myself was unbreakable. Now, I'm starting to see that my power lies in my ability to choose differently and to face my emotions and my circumstances with a clear, present mindset. Mind you, this transformation has not been about becoming a different person overnight; rather, it's about building a new foundation. Every decision I make now rests on the solid ground of that foundation instead of the shaky platform alcohol had given me. The finality of this change, which felt daunting at first, is now a source of comfort. Knowing that I will not return to that cycle, that I will not allow myself to be pulled back, gives me a sense of control and peace that I've never felt before.

I don't expect others to follow my path. I know that not everyone has the same struggles with alcohol that I did. I'm not here to judge those who can drink without falling into the same patterns— my journey is mine alone. I am simply proud that I took the steps I needed to take to reclaim my life and do better for myself and those I love.

Controlling what I can and letting go of what I cannot have become my new mantra. Life will always have its unpredictable moments, and things will always happen that are out of my control, but I now have the clarity to face those moments in a way I never could before.

Now, a year into my sobriety journey, I feel like the fog has lifted. The dust has settled, and I am starting to rebuild, piece by piece, from the remains of my old life. I've learned to appreciate the quiet, the calm, and the beauty of moments that don't need the support of alcohol. I am taking ahead with me the lessons I've learned, the grace I've earned along the way, and the pride that comes from knowing I have stayed true to myself. The love and support from my friends and family have been overwhelming, reminding me that I am not alone in this journey; they're always there with me, supporting me and nudging me ahead. There is a profound peace in surrounding myself with people who have genuine intentions, who love me for who I am, and not for the social version of me that used to come out after a few drinks.

As I move forward in life, I am committed to holding myself to a higher standard than I ever did. Today, I expect better things from and for myself. I don't settle for less because I know I deserve only the best. Sobriety isn't just about avoiding alcohol; it's about embracing a life that is fully mine, a life that isn't blurred by substances or weakened by regret. I am learning to be fully present, to cherish each moment for what it is, without feeling the need to alter it. And though there are days when it's hard, days when the old patterns call out to me, I know that I am stronger now, more than I ever was. I have chosen a new path, a path of clarity and intention, and nothing is going to pull me away from it.

Chapter 7
Boundaries, Growth, and Letting Go

Mess attracts the masses. It's a harsh reality I had to face and one I wrestled with during my lowest moments. When I was at my worst, I had an overflowing circle of "friends." They were drawn to the chaos, the drama, and the endless nights of indulgence that seemed so glamorous at the time. But as I began to climb out of that pit, something interesting happened—those "friends" started to disappear. Now that I've built boundaries, I hear it all the time: "You're different." Well, yes, I am. That was the point.

The version of me that once existed—the one who prioritized everyone else's approval and drowned her own voice in a sea of bad decisions—is gone. Shedding that toxic veil wasn't just necessary; it was life-saving. Letting go of the people who weren't meant to stay in my life has been as transformative as the decision to get sober. My energy is now sacred, reserved only for people and places that align with the healthiest version of myself. And I make no apologies for that.

Protecting my peace is now my full-time

commitment. I stand firm in my decisions, unapologetically choosing what's best for me. My family and true friends understand and respect this, and honestly, that's all I need. Spectators, however, are inevitable. Watching the rise and fall of others seems to be ingrained in human nature, doesn't it? But I've dug myself out of the shadows, and I have no intention of looking back. I refuse to waste my energy entertaining the curiosity of a crowd that isn't genuinely invested in my well-being.

The proof of my growth speaks for itself. Whether it's in my personal life, my professional endeavors, or my relationships, the results are undeniable. I've been working consistently, frequently, and successfully to rebuild myself from the ground up. Each step forward has been a triumph, and no one can take that from me.

Journaling played a huge role in this journey. In the beginning, when I was taking my first shaky steps into sobriety, those private writings were my lifeline. My journal became a safe space to pour out the thoughts and emotions I couldn't yet share with anyone else. Over time, those scattered entries grew into something bigger—a series of chapters that eventually turned into this book. Essentially, you're getting a tongue-in-cheek peek into my diary.

So, welcome. Settle in. Get comfortable with being uncomfortable because this testimony—my years spent trapped in a bottle and my climb back to freedom—is a bumpy ride. But it's real, raw, and mine.

And here's something I've learned along the way: The concept of "going no contact" isn't just for people. It applies to habits, too. Whether it's a behavior, a routine, or even a mindset that's no longer serving you, it's never too late to let it go. It's never too late to choose better. And if my story can teach you anything, let it be this: The hard work of becoming the person you were always meant to be is worth it. Every. Single. Step.

When I began my approach to sobriety, I didn't lead with lofty ideals or grand promises. Instead, I leaned on pragmatic justification, breaking down the reasons I drank and asking myself what I stood to gain by stopping. That practical approach didn't erase the bad chapters of my past, but it replaced them with the likelihood of good for the future. And that was enough to keep me moving forward.

Alcohol had been a constant companion in the mistakes I wish I could undo. It amplified the chances of doomed experiences: regretful tattoos, questionable decisions, avoidable confrontations, and embarrassing moments on social media. There was unnecessary stress and associations with people I now realize weren't meant to be in my life. Sobriety didn't make me perfect, nor did it make me better than anyone else, but it helped me see that I was above some of the chaos I had allowed into my life. My altered sense of self-worth had made space for things I didn't deserve, and I won't let that happen again.

Today, when people from my past—those I've intentionally chosen not to associate with—gossip about me or attempt to make me look bad, I remind myself of one thing: They're trying to steal my progress from an empty house. I don't live there anymore. They can rattle the walls and throw stones at the windows, but it's meaningless because I've moved on.

We all make mistakes; that's part of being human. However, not everyone puts in the work to rectify the choices that led to those mistakes. For me, getting sober was the first step toward reconciliation—not just with others but with myself. And that's why I wrote this book. It's from my heart to yours, a call to open up pathways for hard conversations and personal reflection. It's time to release the stigma of shame surrounding losing our footing in life. Everyone stumbles. What matters is how we get back up.

Our habits don't form overnight, and the process of rebuilding won't happen in a day. But that's okay. We are the authors of our own lives, and the beauty of being the writer is that you can always throw in a positive plot twist. You can take the narrative in a new direction, no matter how deep the old storyline ran.

Sobriety hasn't solved all my problems, and it hasn't wiped the slate clean. But it has simplified my path to an outcome I never thought possible. It has helped me focus on the things that truly matter and let go of what doesn't serve me. And for that, I'll be forever grateful.

Nobody forced me into this decision. Sobriety wasn't something I was dragged into; it was something I had to want with every fiber of my being. I had to want to end the cycle and open myself up to the uncomfortable process of maneuvering through something different. Most of all, I had to want to be a better person, not just for myself but for my children, husband, family, friends, work, and future.

Making that choice meant ripping off the Band-Aid and facing the music, no matter how much it stung. Until you have that epiphany, that deep, internal shift where you know it's time, committed change feels impossible. But once that moment arrives, everything starts to fall into place.

Now, I celebrate this win on a monthly basis, and it's a joy I never expected to feel. Each milestone feels like fuel for the next, and before you know it, the momentum takes over. Looking back, I see the countless opportunities I've had to drink since making this commitment, but instead of regret or longing, I feel an overwhelming sense of pride and power. I didn't give in, not once. That's something no one can take away from me or diminish. It's a pure, undeniable testament to the work I've done, and that accomplishment resonates deeply in my spirit, serving as a source of hope and strength for the days ahead.

Sobriety has become a competition with myself, a game where the only goal is to be better than I was yesterday. It's a game I love playing—and winning—time and again. The support and encouragement from my friends and family have amplified those good feelings because they are the epicenter of my life. Their love and belief in me remind me of why I started this journey in the first place.

There was a time when the highlight of my day was recounting wild stories of how much I drank or how late I stayed up. Those tales used to bring me a strange sense of pride, as if they were badges of honor. Now, those stories have been replaced with ones of calm, successful, loving, and beautiful interactions that enrich my life in ways I couldn't have imagined back then.

During my drinking years, I surrounded myself with people who drank irresponsibly and in excess. I thought we shared a common interest, a bond that brought us closer. In reality, all we shared was something that was poisoning my life. Those connections weren't about camaraderie; they were about enabling a cycle I desperately needed to break.

Choosing sobriety was a deeply personal decision, one I made for myself and no one else. It didn't come with any expectations for the people around me. I didn't need anyone to change with me or for me. This journey was mine alone, and it was done by me, for me. That, in itself, is the most empowering part of it all.

Sobriety isn't a one-size-fits-all solution. For many of us, the journey lies somewhere on the alcoholic misuse spectrum—a space where the pull of old habits is strong, yet the desire for change burns brighter. Navigating that spectrum took work, but I found strategies that helped me realign my life and rediscover my strengths.

Listening to sobriety podcasts became a source of

inspiration, offering voices of people who had walked a similar path. Their stories made me feel less alone. Walking outdoors became another refuge, a way to clear my mind and embrace the stillness I once avoided. Focusing on my mental health gave me the clarity I needed to see my life for what it was and decide what it could become.

A pivotal step was cutting people out of my life who encouraged dysfunction. It wasn't easy, but it was necessary. I realized that healing doesn't just mean stopping harmful behaviors; it means letting go of the environments and relationships that perpetuate them. Leaving certain people and places behind was a hard decision, but it helped me move forward. With each step, I felt the weight lift and my spirit lighten. My life began to transform, setting its frequency to something I can only describe as a sanctuary.

Mindset is everything. Changing the way I think, rerouting my priorities, and lowering my tolerance for negativity became the foundation of my growth. I had to quiet my fears, let go of the habits that had been holding me back, and remember that if I wanted a thriving life, I had to tend to it like a gardener. The choices that once drained my energy and diminished my self-worth were debilitating. Letting them go allowed me to focus on nurturing my own growth.

As I unshackled myself from toxic habits, I began to reclaim my identity. I rediscovered passions I'd neglected, renewed my spirit, and restored my confidence. In their place, I found courage, self-love, and happiness—tools that empowered me to break free from harmful ties and soar to new heights.

With every step forward, I developed strength, resilience, and determination. The further I went, the more I realized I was never truly broken. I was always capable of flourishing, even when I didn't believe it myself.

When we strive to become better, something amazing happens: everything around us begins to improve, too. The positivity we cultivate within ourselves radiates outward, touching our relationships, our work, and our outlook on life. I see it in my own reflection—this new version of me, filled with peace, plans, and hope. I love the woman I am becoming, and I am excited for the journey still ahead.

I protect myself by limiting who and what has access to me. This isn't about arrogance; it's about being conscious, purposeful, and intentional with my energy. I've learned that being around me is a privilege, and I don't say that lightly. It's a realization that comes from valuing my own worth and understanding that not everything or everyone is meant to be part of my journey.

Sometimes, deliverance comes in unexpected ways. For some, it looks like a DWI. For others, it's physical ailments or the loss of friendships that were never meant to last. Whatever form it takes, the lessons are there, waiting for us to recognize them. But it's up to us to approach those lessons with an open mind, allowing them to guide us toward change and betterment.

Elevation requires separation. To rise, I had to separate myself from certain people, habits, and environments. It wasn't easy, but it was necessary. And as hard as those separations were, I am endlessly thankful for the evolution they brought into my life.

Bad chapters can still create great stories. Wrong paths can lead to the right places. Sometimes, losing yourself is the only way to truly find yourself—and that's exactly what happened to me.

The self-work I've done in silence has echoed through every aspect of my life. It's in the way I carry myself, the way I approach challenges, and the way I embrace every part of my journey. I don't try to hide my struggles because those struggles are where my hope was built. For too long, I let pain consume me in silence, but now I am proud to be healing out loud.

Setting the frequency of my life to sanctuary has been one of the most transformative choices I've ever made. I move forward unapologetically, stepping into my power and embracing my highest self. My goal isn't to impress anyone or meet external expectations—it's simply to outdo myself, to grow beyond who I was yesterday.

This is my journey, and I am living it boldly, with purpose and pride. Healing isn't linear, and it isn't always graceful, but it is mine, and I wouldn't trade it for anything.

Chapter 8
The Power of Change and Self-Discovery

Journaling was my lifeline when I first began my walk with sobriety. It wasn't just about getting thoughts out of my head—it became the thread I used to pull myself out of the chaos. What started as a private practice, something just for me, eventually turned into a series of chapters. Those scribbled pages, filled with raw emotion, pain, and growth, are now bound to form this book.

So, here we are. Essentially, you're getting a tongue-in-cheek peek into my diary. Welcome. Settle in, get comfortable with being uncomfortable because this testimony—my years spent in the bottle and the climb out—isn't a smooth ride. It's bumpy, messy, and real. But it's mine.

The concept of "going no contact" isn't just for people. It's applicable to habits, too. And believe me, I've had my share of habits that needed cutting out. Whether it's a routine, a mindset, or a toxic relationship, it's never too late to be better. That realization hit me like a ton of bricks—getting sober didn't magically erase the bad from my past. It didn't wipe the slate clean. But it replaced that past with the likelihood of something better ahead, and that alone made every struggle worth it.

Alcohol wasn't just a drink for me; it was a destructive companion. It increased the chances of doomed experiences, like regrettable tattoos I could never undo, questionable decisions that kept me up at night, avoidable confrontations I'd rather forget, and the embarrassing moments on social media that still make me cringe. It brought unnecessary stress into my life and tied me to people who, frankly, didn't deserve a spot in my world.

I'm not better than anyone. That's not the point. But I am above some of the shit I allowed in my life because of my altered sense of self-worth. For a long time, I didn't value myself enough to set boundaries or say no to things and people that didn't align with who I truly was. I was out of touch with myself, and alcohol made sure of that. But once I decided to get sober, everything started to shift. I started to see my worth in a way I hadn't before.

When people I no longer associate with gossip about me, trying to paint a picture of who I used to be and make me look bad, I remind myself of one thing: they're trying to steal my progress from an empty house. I don't live there anymore. I've moved on, and that's a fact that no one can take away from me.

We all make mistakes. That's part of being human. But not all of us do the hard work to fix what went wrong. I've worked hard, fought through the discomfort, and looked my past square in the face. I've done the work—on myself and with myself. And that's something I'll never apologize for.

This journey, though challenging, has given me the space to finally step into who I was always meant to be. It's not perfect, but it's mine. And I'm proud of that.

I hope this book, from my heart to yours, opens up pathways to hard-hitting conversations and personal reflection that release the stigma of shame surrounding those times when we lose our footing in life. We all fall at some point; it's not about whether we stumble, but about what we do when we get up.

Our habits don't develop overnight, and the rebuilding process doesn't happen in a day. There's no magic switch. But here's the thing: we are the authors of our own lives. We have the power to rewrite our stories, even if it means throwing in a positive plot twist when things seem impossible. For me, getting sober didn't erase all my problems, but it simplified my path to an outcome I never could have imagined. The weight that lifted, the clarity that came—it was all worth it.

If you're struggling, please know this: there is help, and there is a way out. Talk to a friend, a family member, someone at your church, or in a support group. Talk to your doctor or reach out to a hotline. Talk to God, if that's where you find peace. The point is, you don't have to suffer in silence. We are not meant to walk these journeys alone, no matter how isolated you may feel right now.

If you're unsure where to start, there are resources available to guide you. **National Alcohol Hotline**: 1-800-662-HELP (4357).

Remember, you are not alone. And if you decide that today is the day to make a change, know that you can do it. There's a brighter future ahead, one that's waiting for you to step into it. We all deserve to live our best lives, free from the chains of unhealthy habits.

This is your story. And if you're ready, the next chapter can be your best yet.

For a long time, I didn't want to face my truths. Confronting them meant breaking down the illusions I had spent years building around myself. It felt safer to stay in the fog, convinced that the image I'd created was the one I should live by. But over time, I came to understand that the truth was inevitable, and that I was never too old to start doing the right thing. However, I was too old to keep doing things that clearly weren't working.

So, I inspected my behaviors, examined the patterns I'd allowed, and made a weighted decision to change. I created two lists: one for the things I needed to stop doing, and the other for the things I wanted to start doing. The "stop doing" list was the hardest—it meant letting go of familiar habits, even the ones that felt comfortable. The "to-do" list was the opposite; the exciting part—the new actions that would shape a healthier future.

I learned quickly that rushing to accomplish my goal wasn't the answer. My nervous system screamed for immediate results, a sense of urgency that only made things feel more overwhelming. But when I slowed down, took it day by day, the panic I initially felt started to fade. The world didn't need to move at lightning speed for me to make progress. In fact, slowing down allowed me to feel grounded and present in the moment, something I hadn't known how to do for a long time.

There's no perfect way to live, and there are certainly no perfect people. I had to embrace the beautiful unknown, a journey filled with the messiness of growth and change. As I incorporated logical, healthy choices into my life, I began to feel hope again. Hope for the future, hope that I could do better by others and by myself.

The decision to commit to that path wasn't just a choice; it became a devotion. I no longer wanted to make visits to dark valleys. I didn't want to remain in the shadows of uncertainty and self-doubt. Instead, I wanted to thrive in the positive peaks, to rise above the struggles, and embrace the light of a life worth living.

The love I have for my family and true friends has been unwavering. They've supported me in ways I never imagined possible, and I've been incredibly blessed to feel that same love in return during this journey. It's that love, that mutual respect and understanding, that has carried me through the hardest moments. It's the reason I keep going.

This journey has been about more than sobriety—it's been about embracing the truths, no matter how uncomfortable, and choosing a path of peace and positivity. And I'm committed to walking it every single day.

Betterment doesn't equate to perfection, but I'm thankful to be skipping rocks on exponentially improved and peaceful waters. For someone like me, stillness—both physically and psychologically—does not come naturally. It's always been easier to keep moving, keep going, without taking the time to truly assess the path ahead. But in recent years, I've learned that slowing down isn't a sign of weakness; it's a crucial component of cognitive and character development. Taking the time to reflect, to dissect where I've been and where I'm going, has been one of the most important pieces of my healing.

Old energy has been cleared, and in its place, new ways of thinking have taken root. Sobriety has granted me the clarity to rethink my choices, reframe my mindset, and ultimately evolve. It's been about processing the regrets tied to my mistakes, acknowledging them without letting them define me, and choosing to forge forward regardless of my past. Progress is often quiet, subtle, and sometimes difficult to measure, but in these small steps, I've found pride in the fact that I didn't give up.

My healing has come with sitting in discomfort, allowing myself to feel and absorb lessons for as long as it takes. I used to fear the discomfort of facing my own truth, but I now know it's where the growth happens. And sobriety gave me that clarity—clarity to see that discomfort isn't something to run from but something to lean into.

Before you judge someone for their habits, I challenge you: put down your phone for 24 hours. When you feel the urge to reach for it, that's what it feels like. Addiction, bad habits, old patterns—they don't look the same on everyone, and they certainly don't feel the same. What comes easy to some people doesn't come easy to everyone. There are things I used to say, ways I used to think that I no longer agree with. There are things I used to do that I no longer do. And that doesn't make me two-faced; it simply means I'm growing.

I've changed my fundamental interests made room for new things, new people, and new environments that align with who I truly am. I've learned to focus on what I really want out of life, not what I thought I was supposed to want. And with that shift, I now feel free. I realized that the cage I once lived in was never built by external forces—it was objectively measured through my own thoughts and habits.

I've become a silent architect of my life, shaping how I interact with the world and how I pursue my goals. Each decision I make now, each step forward, is a deliberate act of creation, not a reaction. And in this space of intentional living, I feel a peace I didn't know was possible.

I believe the enemy of better decision-making in my life was isolation. For so long, I kept my struggles to myself, convinced that no one could understand or that I was somehow weak for feeling the way I did. But over time, I realized that talking about my struggles has been a vital key to my healing. It's not just about me anymore; sharing my story has the potential to help someone else who's fighting their own battles. Sometimes, the simple act of speaking the truth can be the first step toward freedom.

I wasn't drinking every day, but when I did consume alcohol, I was abusing the limits I had set for myself. It wasn't just the frequency; it was the reckless decisions I made when I had a drink in my hand. I chose to get honest with myself, and that honesty led me to a hard truth: altering my decision-making skills for the sake of temporary comfort often resulted in negative outcomes. I wasn't willing to accept the risks those consequences brought anymore.

For me, discernment was about being able to spot the problems as they arose, then working toward fixing them. I spent years thinking the habits I had were making me better—thinking that the coping mechanisms I'd adopted were helping me grow. But in reality, they were slowly killing my personality, my moral compass, my self-respect. And I firmly believe it would have eventually eroded my body, my beautiful family, my friendships, and my professional drive. It was a silent destruction, one I hadn't fully understood until I took a step back.

When I decided to change, I took the pressure off myself to perform for the world. I stopped worrying about being judged or ridiculed for showing up as my real, authentic self. The moment I let go of that fear, something miraculous happened: my life became infused with true light. I wasn't just existing anymore—I was living, fully and unapologetically.

There is something so freeing about owning the joy of who you truly are. It's in doing the things that nourish your emotional, mental, and physical health. I learned that joy isn't found in trying to meet the expectations of others; it's found in honoring who you are and embracing the things that bring you peace and happiness. And once I made that shift, my world became brighter—more vibrant—than I ever thought possible.

It wasn't easy, but it was worth it. Taking off the mask and showing up as myself has brought me more peace than I ever expected.

Getting drunk used to be my escape. It was my way of fleeing from the chaos in my mind, from the pain I didn't want to face. But one day, something inside of me clicked. I asked myself, why would I want to escape my own life? I had spent so many years harboring pain, sabotaging myself, letting it poison the beautiful things I had around me. The relationships, the opportunities, the love—why was I letting them slip through my fingers?

It was time to stop running. I needed to allow myself to bask in the beauty of the things that mattered most—my family, my children, my marriage, my friends, my career, and all of my accomplishments. These were the treasures of my life, and I was finally ready to embrace them. For so long, I felt unworthy of happiness because of the hurtful experiences that had weighed me down. That belief was a bear I wrestled with for years, but I can finally say that I've let go of it.

Stepping out from under the crushing weight of external judgments has been the most liberating part of my journey. No longer living to meet other people's expectations has allowed me to stand in my power, fueled by my own internal influence. And that's what intoxicates me now—the power I've reclaimed, the peace I've found, and the love I feel for the life I've built.

I've fallen in love with my life. For the first time, I'm fully present, soaking in the joy of the simple moments. I've purposely positioned myself to focus on the things that bring ease to my peace. And as I look forward, I plan to proceed as though success is inevitable, because I know

now that it is.

The root of my suffering was attachment. I clung to habits, mindsets, and routines that no longer served a purpose for positive progression. But once I relied on my own strength to detach from those toxic cycles, I found extraordinary success waiting on the other side.

I didn't want to look back on my life as a series of vacuous decisions. I wanted to make things right. I wanted to make things better. I wanted to make things simpler. Downsizing isn't just for houses; it's for mindsets and environmental factors, too. Everything needed an overhaul, a revamp, a rebirth. I flipped it all upside down, emptied the contents, and started again.

I was done filling the void. It was time to recalibrate the way I lived—to manage my life with boundaries, discipline, and intention. The list of crises that had gone unaddressed in my life was long, but I was ready to take it on.

This book isn't about appropriating pain; it's about inspiring healing. It's about doing more, being more, and giving yourself permission to flourish. It's a stepping stone, a launchpad, a strategic plan for action. It's about releasing the cycle that lets your soul wither away, trapped in the bottle or bound by other destructive habits.

Healing is an active process, and this journey has been my recalibration—not just of my habits but of my life, my purpose, and my peace.

Mindset is everything in healing. It's the main character in the story of recovery, growth, and transformation. If someone came to you, expressing the same things you've been feeling, what would you say to comfort them? What words would you offer to help them see their worth, their potential, their ability to overcome? Now ask yourself—what's keeping you from showing yourself that same care?

It's time to show up for yourself with the same kindness, love, and compassion that you'd show to anyone else. You deserve it, and I'm here to tell you—you are worthy of it.

I've found that self-discovery is at the heart of my healing journey. It's been a constant evolution, an unraveling of who I truly am beneath all the layers of habits and denial. Every fiber of my body would scream at me when I was hungover. I felt debilitated, sluggish, hopeless—trapped in a cycle I couldn't break. And in those moments, the empty anthem would play over and over in my head: *I promised I wouldn't do this again.* But I would. And I did. For years.

Brunette and Boozy Free

The confusion that clouded my judgment slowly cleared when I got sober. My brain, for the first time in a long while, felt logical and sharp. I could see clearly now that these behaviors were wrong—that the path I was on was toxic. But even though my logical mind knew the truth, the habitual reflex to escape, to numb, was always there, whispering for me to "come out and play" as soon as the opportunity arose.

It was a merry-go-round, but the ride stopped being fun. Instead, it became a spiraling descent into a place I didn't recognize, a dangerous place for my spirit to get lost. I was embarrassed. I was in denial. I desperately wanted to be the fun, vivacious person I thought I was supposed to be, like others seemed to be when they drank. But what I didn't realize at the time was that my body and my brain were exhausted. They were pleading for a change, and I had to listen.

I needed to redefine the role alcohol played in my life. It wasn't easy, and it took time, but eventually, the fog started to lift. What became clear was that my path was unsustainable, and I had to make a choice. The turning point for me came when I saw the change in friends who had also chosen sobriety. They were thriving, and I realized that *I* could thrive too.

I've never heard anyone say they regret getting sober. Have you? But I've heard countless stories of people regretting how much they drank the night before. The weight of those small regrets, those moments of fleeting joy followed by overwhelming shame, added up. And eventually, they became big signs to me—signs that I couldn't ignore anymore.

The thought of living a life without alcohol was terrifying, no doubt. But the thought of continuing down the path I was on was far scarier. And so, I gave up one thing—the thing that had been holding me captive—for something so much better. The rewards were abundant, and they came in ways I never expected. I received peace, clarity, strength, and an authentic connection to my life and my loved ones.

It's been a journey of rediscovery. Every day, I'm reminded of how far I've come, and how much more is waiting for me on the other side of sobriety.

My self-control became my strength, and calmness became my mastery. Gone are the days of wishing for better, because the better has arrived—and it's more brilliant than I ever could have imagined. The truth is, just because you've been doing something a certain way for so long doesn't mean it's impossible to change. In fact, it's thrilling to throw in a positive plot twist, to rewrite the narrative of your life in ways you never thought possible.

But I won't sugarcoat it—the beginning wasn't sparkling and easy. It was far from that. It was shitty. It was hard. The emotional and psychological toll of your body going through a complete reset is no small feat. Breakups are hard, and retraining my mind to deconstruct the relationship I had built with alcohol felt, at times, impossible.

There were moments when I questioned if it was worth it. But then, I made a choice: each time I committed to seeing how it felt to go to dinner with friends and not drink, to go on a vacation with my family and not drink, to celebrate a birthday and not drink, to attend a concert or sporting event and not drink—I felt a shift. It wasn't immediate, and it wasn't easy, but slowly, over time, it began to develop into my new social muscle memory.

Each experience, each moment without alcohol, was a small victory. It wasn't about being perfect; it was about proving to myself that I could be present, fully and without distraction, in the moments that really mattered. And over time, those small victories added up. They built the foundation for the life I'm living now—a life where I'm not at the mercy of a bottle, but rather, at the helm of my own ship.

It's amazing how much power we hold when we stop letting old habits define us. It's amazing what happens when we choose to be the authors of our own stories. I may have started in a place of struggle, but now I stand in a place of mastery, and that journey has been worth every single step.

It became a contest, a battle between my competing thoughts and judgments. For so long, I was torn, unsure of what I truly wanted. But in the end, I got sober because I wanted a better life. And I stay sober because I got one. The clarity that sobriety brought with it was undeniable.

I stopped feeding my anxieties and insecurities, and instead, I chose to nurture myself. That decision produced something I hadn't expected: a force field of protection against negativity, low productivity, and uninspiring experiences. It wasn't easy at first; it's always easier to do things that reflect disdain for yourself, to fall into old patterns that keep you small and unseen. But every time I chose to demonstrate habits of love and care for myself, everything else slowly began to fall into place.

I no longer felt the need to be accommodating, small, quiet, convenient, or digestible for others. I realized I didn't have to shrink myself to fit into the world's expectations. This wasn't just about stopping the alcohol—it was about stopping the madness I had allowed into my life altogether. I was tired of being at the mercy of every negative thought and destructive habit.

I became rooted in the fact that past traumas, or the daily stressors of life, didn't give me an excuse to behave poorly. It wasn't a justification anymore; it was a realization that my past didn't have to dictate my future. Alcohol had been a major part of a dysfunctional pattern in my life, and it created many unpleasant memories along the way. But now, it serves as a powerful reminder of what I don't want to be.

I've accepted the notion that it's not selfish to have different priorities for my life. I'm allowed to want something better. I'm allowed to choose peace, growth, and authenticity over what's comfortable or familiar. And in that choice, I've found a sense of freedom I never thought was possible. I've learned that the life I deserve is the one I create, and I'm no longer willing to settle for anything less.

Chapter 9
Choosing a Life of Clarity and Strength

My decision to get sober wasn't an abrupt process. It was a slow-burning build-up, a yearning to seek harmony in my life by untangling the willfully laced smidges of cognitive dissonance tied to my irresponsible choices. I had to face the truth, piece by piece, and dismantle the justifications that kept me stuck.

I found that many of my problems began to fade when I removed certain people and eliminated habits that no longer served me. The clarity that came with those choices was undeniable. I realized I couldn't simply trim the branches of my issues; I had to heal the root to save the tree. Building my sober foundation on my wins, rather than my shame, became a cornerstone of my focus. Concentrating on my strengths and reminding myself, *"I don't live like that anymore,"* helped me celebrate my resilience and the progress I was making.

Starting with positive thoughts instead of drowning in past failures gave me a clearer vision of my future. It allowed me to define and frame out my goals in a way that felt achievable. There were moments when the overwhelming ledge of negativity nearly pushed me over the edge, but instead of succumbing, I collected small wins along the way. Those wins, though minor at first, built momentum and gave me something to hold onto.

Taking accountability for my actions was an essential part of the journey. Wandering into wise remorse helped me acknowledge the impact of my choices without sinking into shame. Shame didn't change things—it only kept me down. I knew I needed to move forward, not stay stuck in the past.

Replacing drinking with activities I genuinely enjoyed became a turning point. I found joy in living my life fully and intentionally rather than numbing myself with alcohol. Sobriety is a journey with many paths, and I discovered the approach that worked best for me. It wasn't about following a prescribed method; it was about finding what resonated and sticking with it.

Some disconnections have been an absolute blessing. I now know I can't live the life I have today if I drink, and I love this new chapter exponentially more. Having an unhealthy relationship with alcohol was like a one-way ticket to hell for me, and I'm proud of myself for recognizing the signs and having the courage to evoke change.

The truth is, I had two choices: quit drinking or keep drinking. Both options hurt. But only one of them yielded good results. And I chose the path that led to healing, clarity, and the life I always deserved.

Strength has been born out of my weaknesses, and vulnerability has paved the way for self-acceptance. I no longer feel the need to validate myself by clinging to old norms that no longer serve me. Choosing to experience a better way of life—one that nourishes both my body and my mind—has been the ultimate reward.

My focus has shifted to the simple yet fulfilling things in life: spending quality time with family, enjoying outings with friends, traveling with my husband, supporting causes I believe in within my community, and building my business. Clean living has given me a clean canvas, a fresh start, and a renewed outlook on my future.

When I began this journey, I wasn't sure I was up for the challenge. Coming out of the descent into my darkness felt overwhelming. But little by little, I grew stronger—and as I did, everything around me became stronger too. Brick by brick, I rebuilt and renovated the things that truly mattered to me. I allowed the toxic inhabitants of my time and mind to fall away, and the ripples of that decision have echoed through every aspect of my life.

Is drinking alcohol bad? For me, it was. Do I miss it? I don't miss the negative experiences, the low-grade friendships, the painful hangovers, or the empty feelings that always followed a big day of drinking. Alcohol, for me, was an energy vampire. It drained the positive potential from my life, leaving behind a wake of poor decisions and a disregard for reality. The direct correlation between my improved life and my decision to get sober is undeniable.

Today, I no longer feel like I'm spinning out of control. I feel secure, grounded, and in charge of my own life. Sobriety has given me clarity—every day, all day. That clarity has also sharpened my perspective, giving me a low tolerance for anything that doesn't align with my growth. I reject what doesn't serve my peace and stand firm in my dedication to doing what's best for my well-being.

Everyone's journey is their own, and I firmly believe in respecting that truth. But for me, getting sober was the decision that transformed my life. I've learned to embrace simplicity, stand in my strength, and focus on the things that truly matter. And for that, I'll always be grateful.

Sobriety isn't for everyone, and it's not something I push onto others. It was simply the step I needed to take to save myself. Under the influence, I was magnetized to low-grade experiences, people, and situations. Now, I've attracted better energy and cultivated deeper connections rooted in quality intention. I'm no longer chasing outside validation or seeking comfort at the bottom of a bottle.

Setting out on the path of change meant actively doing the work to confront the ugliness in my habits—the ones dragging me further from the life I was meant to live. It's been nothing short of an overhaul evolution. Alcohol illuminated my wounds and gave me false power, but sobriety has given me a life richer than my wildest dreams.

The journey has been about more than quitting drinking; it's been about working to conquer the innermost toxicity that chained me to harmful old habits. Over time, that work has transformed into a healed reflexology, where the absence of alcohol is now the headliner of my daily life. It's no longer a battle—it's a choice I make every day with confidence and pride.

Most of the fight in the beginning was about getting my mind right. A significant part of that work included forgiving myself. Holding onto the ugly memories of the things I'd said or done under the influence was like a wincing pain every time they resurfaced. Forgiving myself didn't happen all at once. It's not something that happens overnight. It's a slow progression, a gradual release.

There were days when I'd take two steps forward and four steps back. But even in those moments of setback, I grew stronger. With time, I became more resilient. I didn't always see it, but I could feel it—the heaviness of guilt and shame slowly starting to fade as I continued to put in the work.

I stopped pouring my energy into toxicity, and that included my own negative thoughts about myself. Forgiveness became my greatest act of self-love. By allowing myself the space and time to heal, I created room for a life filled with peace, clarity, and intention. And with each passing day, I've learned that the weight of the past doesn't have to define my future.

Practicing self-care and telling my broken heart that it was okay to take a break, to remember how to smile again wasn't always easy. There were moments when the darkness felt overwhelming, but I pushed through. I realized that the longer I dwelled in the heartache, the more it festered and grew. It was difficult, but I had to leave it alone. I honored my emotions and allowed myself to feel them fully, but I refused to keep circling back to the same pain.

I knew I couldn't keep obsessing over what had happened. Forgiving myself didn't erase the past or make everything magically okay. It didn't absolve me of the responsibility for my negative actions, nor did it let me forget the embarrassing moments that came with them. Instead, forgiveness meant accepting that what's done is done. It meant admitting there was no rewind button and realizing the only way forward was to regain control of my life by following my soul to the peace it deserved.

I broke down my fears of facing my feelings and reclaiming who I am—on my own terms. I stopped seeking answers in the bottle and instead turned inward. The one thing I was most afraid to do—confronting myself—became the very thing that changed everything. That bravery led me to rediscover the light I thought I had lost.

Today, I feel grounded in good things. I've rebuked the bare minimum and embraced a life built on intentionality and self-respect. I changed, but that was always the point. I firmly believe that if I do better, better will come. So far, that belief has proven true. The work we do on ourselves isn't just for us—it becomes a gift to everyone around us. That realization is powerful.

I've normalized peace in my life because suffering is

not an achievement. I decided what I wanted and became unavailable to dead cycles that kept me stuck. I no longer use my pain as an excuse for poor behavior. The shift inside me has reflected outward, and the alignment I've created is evident in my daily life.

Believe it or not, some disconnections serve as blessings in disguise. Trust the magic of new beginnings. I've corrected myself, redirected myself, and created a sense of confident protection against falling back into habits that would derail my energy, time, or progress. My journey isn't about perfection but about growth. And in that growth, I've found peace and purpose.

Sometimes, it felt like my relationship with alcohol was breaking me. But when I was ready to put the pieces back together, every shattered part of me found a new purpose and a new place within my sobriety. I discovered the courage to rebuild, to redefine strength, and to realize that I wasn't broken—I was breaking through.

I took the time to consider my past mistakes and evaluate what my future could look like without alcohol. At first, it was difficult to imagine because it was unknown territory. The uncertainty and doubts that came with attempting to straighten out my faults were overwhelming. Yet, I already knew the outcomes of my alcohol-induced choices. The lessons from that "curriculum" were predictable, and I figured it was almost a guarantee that anything would be better than staying in that compromised state of mind.

Starting my sobriety journey was hard in the beginning, but the impact has been nothing short of legendary. My happiness and the longevity of my life have become paramount priorities, regardless of how that looks to others. I wanted to be saved from a path of destruction, so I saved myself. I fixed the parts of me that were a problem and protected the parts that were not.

Along the way, I've encountered people who haven't appreciated my changes. They've held on to an old image of me tied to my old habits. But I haven't let that stop me from evolving. Restricting my energy from certain situations has become essential because my peace is more important than attention. With a clear head at all times, I've also been able to distinguish between people genuinely checking on me and those simply checking if they still have access to me.

Upping my self-care has been transformative. It's shown me what is truly meant for me and what isn't. Sobriety gave me the power to change my life and to move in the direction I wanted to go. I'm no longer revolving in circles; I'm evolving moving forward. I'm revolting against anything rooted in disingenuous motives or anything that could lead me back to an unhealthy mindset.

I've mastered survival mode, and now it's time to live. I write this book not to sway others in their lifestyle choices but to respect the sonder—the shared humanity and struggles—that resonates within us all. Everyone battles something, but not everyone talks about it. For me, getting rid of what was holding me back opened up opportunities to chase the things I truly wanted: a healthy mind, an improved body, a happy family, true friendships, and professional productivity.

This journey has been about more than sobriety—it's been about becoming who I was always meant to be.

Chapter 10
The Final Step: Embracing the Gift of Now

Have you ever had a gut feeling that you were meant for more? What's your *more*? For years, I ignored that feeling. I was stuck in a cycle that drained me of the very potential I knew deep down I was capable of reaching.

In the aftermath of drinking, my nervous system felt like it was being hunted for sport. My heart would race with relentless palpitations, waves of cold and hot sweats would surge through my body, and I'd fixate on gobs of unhealthy food as the only solution during my hangovers. The tangled web of spotty recalls—what I had said, what I had done—tormented me long after the alcohol had left my system. I felt lower than low, trapped in a habit that held tight to my throat.

But then, something changed. I decided to see off the evil tentacles holding me in despair and denial. I had to let go, or I would continue to be dragged along. It was time to ask the hard questions: What was alcohol really bringing to my life? What was it doing to me—internally and externally? Was it truly making me better? Was it actually enhancing the happy moments I had?

The answers were painfully obvious. Something that felt so horrible the next day couldn't possibly be good for me. It was reckless and irresponsible that it took me 20 years to realize that, but I'm grateful I finally did. Enough was enough. No more excuses. No more waiting for the "right time"—after a planned gathering with friends or after a particular moment in life passed. Enough.

It was time to stand, deal, and heal. This wasn't about admitting defeat; it was about claiming my worth. For the first time, I truly believed I deserved a beautiful, better life. This was a rebellion against the lackluster treatment I had been putting myself through. It was a chance to rebuild and start again.

Now, I look back at my moments of dark descent not as something that happened *to* me but as something that happened *for* me. Those struggles shaped the person I am today. What I needed couldn't be found at the bottom of a bottle. It had to come from me. Only I could give myself the care, love, and respect I deserved. And so, I did.

The complexities of how life's stressors affect each of us are immeasurable, but facing each day with a clear head has allowed me to see through the falsified fog that alcohol once brought into my life. My devotion to alcohol was an intentional infliction of negativity—a ticket to a perilous playground, a blank check for trouble.

I've always admired my capacity to dream, but the changes that brought positive results came from taking action. Getting to know my true self has been a profound transformation. Emerging from beneath the cloak I had been buried under, I learned a powerful truth: Not every closed door is locked. Sometimes, you just have to push.

At the beginning of my sober path, I mistakenly equated the peace I was feeling with boredom. I had conditioned myself to adapt to the chaos that existed in my head, and without it, I felt unsettled. But soon, I realized that peace wouldn't kill me—though I was certain that continuing to drink eventually could.

The havoc I had inflicted on my body over time was bound to catch up with me, and that was not a fate I wanted to meet. Luckily, no long-term health issues resulted from my choices, but I've seen countless friends lose their battles to this beast. It's a harsh reality that reminds me of how precious and fragile life is.

Life, when approached with the right mindset, is bountiful. At times, it's made up of a series of delicate choices—choices that shape our experiences and our futures. If finding peace makes me boring, then so be it because peace has given me more than I could have imagined: Better health, more money in the bank, sharper thinking, and the ability to show up as a better mother, wife, and friend. Peace has given me energy, clarity, and freedom from the fear of having to embark on yet another apology tour.

Sobriety has been my gateway to a better life, and the clarity it has brought me feels like a long-overdue gift. It's not about perfection—it's about living with intention and showing up for the life I've always deserved.

But this book isn't called *"Brunette and Boring"* because the misconception that sobriety equals boredom should be secondary to the elevated life I've given myself because of it. What some people think is fun isn't always fun, and what some people think is boring isn't always boring. I've lived both sides of the coin, and for my life, the results I've seen from flipping the script have been all the validation I need.

You know who's going through a lot right now? Literally everyone. This book isn't meant to shame anyone into giving up drinking; it's about spreading encouragement—encouragement to revolt against toxic habits, environments, or people who don't contribute to the positive progression of your life. It's about taking a long, honest look at yourself, holding yourself accountable, and taming the demons that hold you back.

It's about letting go of the blinding fears of change in order to take control and limit the things that hurt you. Change is scary, but staying in a cycle of pain and negativity is scarier.

This journey isn't about perfection. It's about empowerment, evolution, and strength. It's about choosing to surround yourself with positivity and pursuing favorable outcomes by detaching from the associations that keep you tethered to negativity.

Sobriety, for me, has been a tool for transformation. It's shown me what's possible when I prioritize my well-being and actively work toward a better version of myself. This chapter, this book, and this life are not about being boring. They're about finding the courage to rewrite the narrative, to own my choices, and to step into a life full of purpose and possibility.

In the early months of my sobriety, I used to be incredibly worried that people would see me holding a "drink" and mistake it for an alcoholic beverage. I felt this compulsion to explain that it wasn't, in fact, a "real" drink. Mocktails these days look remarkably similar to those that contain alcohol, and I found myself overthinking what others might assume.

Slowly but surely, I became more comfortable. I started ordering my sparkling water with lime without feeling the need to clarify. Over time, I realized that most people weren't paying acute attention to what I was drinking. And if they were, the real question was why they were so vested in what I had in my cup instead of focusing on their own choices.

That realization was pivotal for me. It's a reminder that has helped me navigate countless social situations. Mocktails are nothing to be embarrassed about. Acting out of pocket with cocktails? That's where my embarrassment truly lived.

There's no shame in taking care of yourself and prioritizing the things that give you what you need for a positive, fruitful life. The opinions of others—those fleeting, often unimportant judgments—won't slow the improved progress that comes from the care you put into yourself. This journey is yours, and what's in your cup is just a small piece of the bigger picture.

Sometimes, leveling up requires isolation, separation, and extreme focus. I had to allow myself to outgrow and depart from certain practices in my life with a gentle sort of ruthlessness. Growth was what I sought, but I wasn't fully prepared for the discomfort that came with wanting more than the small box others—and sometimes myself—had placed me in.

It felt unnatural at first not to meet up with friends for drinks, but as time passed, I found my stride. I began showing up for concerts, galas, travels, movies, dinners, lunches, and celebrations with friends and family, all without alcohol being an accessory. Bar hopping was no longer on the itinerary, but what I discovered beyond those bar doors was a world more vast and vibrant than I had ever known.

For me, getting wasted was wasting my potential—and running the risk of losing everything I had worked so hard for. As a business owner, I've learned to weigh risks against returns, and it became clear that continuing down that path wasn't worth it. I had to get out of my own way and break the cycle. My mind was either going to break me or build me, and I chose to let it build. The pressures of life didn't change, but my choices did.

I stopped sifting through the red flags and committed to doing the work. Did I believe I could do it? Not entirely. Did I know I needed to do it? Without question. Simplicity became my goal, and from that, simplicity grew bigger and became more beautiful. Those blooms replaced the insecurities that had kept me tethered to the fear of failing.

Even in the hardest moments, I reminded myself not to settle for less just because I was too impatient to wait for better. Personal perspective is unique, and it counts. Nothing works unless you do. Stepping into the unknown was terrifying, but staying in the distorted reality I had created was even scarier.

I didn't want to keep missing out on my life by claiming I was "getting it together" while failing to follow through with any real actions. The resistance I thought I'd face ultimately turned out to exist only in my mind. Breaking that toxic pattern was worth every loss I experienced in the process because the close relationships and meaningful experiences I've gained far outweigh the blurry ghosts of my old life.

I am no longer anchored, bound to the bottle, and having my mind hijacked by alcohol. Now, I feel free—free to soar in a clear sky, hopeful and confident that I'm on the right path to a better destination.

During my tumultuous years of drinking, I felt like I was held captive in my own body. It was as if I were imprisoned by my choices, unable to break free. There are no bad consequences to quitting drinking, but there are countless terrible outcomes if you don't. I had to take charge of my thoughts and adopt the mindset that things are only as significant as I decide they are. That perspective applied to both the good and the bad.

Inflammation, a puffy face, feelings of self-deprecating inadequacy, and perplexing anxiety were the predictable consequences awaiting me after a night of drinking. These symptoms weren't just physical—they built a fortress of doom that surrounded my mind and spirit, keeping me stuck in a cycle I desperately needed to escape.

One of the most challenging goodbyes I ever faced occurred when I made the commitment to stop drinking. It was a difficult farewell, not because I doubted it was the right choice, but because I knew it was necessary for building a better life. Staying in my relationship with alcohol meant clinging to the hope that things would magically change—while tolerating its hurtful effects and accepting minimal effort from myself to avoid the pain of letting go.

Although departing from alcohol was painful, it ultimately led to my healing. Conversely, staying would have perpetuated a cycle of hurt, deepening my wounds and keeping me tethered to a toxic pattern. I chose to stop drinking not because I didn't love the habit but because I loved myself more.

I had to train my boundaries and remind myself that it's never too late to change my routine, my focus, and my core interests. I had to believe in my own power to change, to get myself unstuck. I had to nourish my mind and love myself enough to break the cycle. I realized that the relationship I had with myself set the tone for every decision I made moving forward.

Worrying was worshipping the problem, so I knew I needed to take action. I firmly believed in the process, and over time, I learned that self-validation would always triumph over self-judgment. Slowly but surely, my vision became my reality.

I didn't want to keep putting off better choices for "later" because later always turned into never. Later, I would lose interest. Later, the day would turn into night. Later, I would grow older. I knew that life would go by, and I would regret not doing something when I had the chance. So I stopped waiting for later, and I chose now. That choice changed everything.

Life is a fleeting dance, a delicate balance of moments that unfold before us, never to return in quite the same way again. Each second is precious, a gift we often overlook in the rush of daily living.

Regret is a bitter pill to swallow. It is a weight that

bears down upon the soul, reminding us of missed chances and opportunities left untouched. I didn't want to live my life carrying that burden. I didn't want to let the fear of failure or the comfort of complacency hold me back from experiencing the fullness of what life has to offer.

I wanted to seize the moments as they came, with my heart open and my arms outstretched, ready to embrace the possibilities that lay before me. In the end, it's not the things I did that I regret most. It's the things I left undone—the words unspoken, the risks not taken, the opportunities ignored—that would ultimately weigh me down.

This journey has been about more than sobriety. It has been about reclaiming my life, finding my purpose, and stepping boldly into the unknown. It's been about learning to value the fleeting beauty of life's dance and giving myself permission to live fully, deeply, and without reservation. As I close this book, I carry forward the lessons I've learned and the strength I've gained. I choose to live with intention, to honor the moments that make up my days, and to embrace the infinite possibilities that await because life is too short to live with regrets and too beautiful not to live with hope.

Made in the USA
Columbia, SC
28 March 2025